Stop the Bullying

A handbook for teachers

KEN RIGBY

Pembroke Publishers Limited

Pembroke Publishers
538 Hood Road
Markham, Ontario, Canada L3R 3K9
www.pembrokepublishers.com

Distributed in the U.S. by Stenhouse Publishers
477 Congress Street
Portland, ME 04101
www.stenhouse.com

This edition is adapted from a book originally published in 2001 by The Australian Council for Educational Research Ltd.

National Library of Canada Cataloguing in Publication Data

Rigby, Ken
   Stop the bullying: a handbook for teachers

1st Canadian ed.
Includes bibliographical references and index.
ISBN 1-55138-137-0

   1. Bullying — Prevention. I. Title.

LB3013.3.R54 2001   371.5'8   C2001-901394-9

Acknowledgments
I am enormously indebted to the thousands of children, teachers and parents who, over the last 12 years, have shared with me their concerns about school bullying, their ideas about what can be done about it, and their heartfelt hope that there will come a day when bullying simply doesn't happen.

   There are many people who have kindly read through the text of this handbook and offered me good advice and encouragement. I would especially like to thank Ms Karen Kitchen, Student Attendance Counsellor – Special Projects, Education Department of South Australia; Ms Alison Soutter, Senior Education Officer, NSW Department of Education and Training; and Ms Jenny Blake, Acting Senior Education Officer, Student Services Branch, Education Services Directorate Education, Queensland, for their perceptive comments. Their expertise and working knowledge of the needs of school personnel in addressing the problem has been much appreciated. They have helped me to write a better book. However, they must not be held in any way accountable for any errors, misjudgments or personal opinions that may disturb or challenge the reader. These are mine and mine alone.

Ken Rigby
www.education.unisa.edu.au/bullying/

Editor: Mignon Turpin, Reina Zatylny
Text design: Egan-reid Ltd., Jay Tee Graphics Ltd.
Cover Design: Chris Payne, CPT Design

Printed and bound in Canada
9 8 7 6 5 4 3 2

CONTENTS

PREFACE

A number of years ago, I was fortunate enough to be part of a major research project initiated by the Toronto Board of Education. The Board was concerned about the increasing incidents of bullying, and asked various departments to collaborate in the investigation of the effects that bullying might have on the self-esteem and achievement of students in schools. Student Support Services and the Research Department approached me in my capacity as Drama Department Co-ordinator to design strategies that teachers, administrators and support staff could use to help students who, for some reason, were the target of unfair treatment. The researchers, social workers and psychologists were interested in finding out how the intervention of drama could provide safe and relevant (although imagined) contexts for the exploration of the complex issue of bullying.

Dramatising Bullying

With the support of the Curriculum Department, I established a student theatre company that was to research, write, produce and tour a play for younger audiences on the theme of bullying. This company of secondary school senior level Dramatic Arts students began researching the material for their play by interacting with elementary students in drama sessions that I organized in various schools. In these drama groups, the elementary and secondary school students explored together, through role-playing, the stories of characters in novels and short stories who themselves had encountered the meanness and misery of bullying. During the drama, the students played various roles taken from these books: parents, elders, social workers, friends, advisors, and journalists. In these roles, they were able to empathize with the situation that the victims of bullying found themselves in, and were able to uncover some of the feelings that these characters were experiencing in the bullying situation. After the drama sessions, the students analyzed the choices that the characters had made and often reflected on their own situations, personal experiences and feelings, comparing them to the ones they had encountered in the stories. The articulate and sensitive secondary school students were powerful role models in these discussions with the younger students, helping them to gain insight to their feelings associated with an imbalance of power in relationships, and to understand the importance of the implications of people's actions, words, and choices that are available to those who are being treated unfairly.

Throughout my work with these students, their messages were consistent and clear. They could not manage bullying alone. They were tired of being told by adults to "go away and work it out". They were more afraid than ever when they were asked "to ignore it". They were angry when some people suggested that they might just as well "fight back", and they were frustrated that the persistent problem of bullying in their lives was misunderstood or not taken seriously by many of parents, teachers and other adults. They longed for schools and community centres to establish policies, procedures and programs that could eliminate bullying from their lives.

Understanding Bullying

I was aware of what I needed as I facilitated this work with these students. I wanted a book that could inform me about bullying, define what it is and what it is not, summarize the research, outline the cycles of bullying and suggest the different kinds of responses. I wanted a resource that I could recommend to teachers and parents that would provide them with some understanding about why bullying happens and give them ideas about actions that they could take to counter bullying. I needed to have at my fingertips a summary of intervention methods for all people involved in the discussion about this complex issue.

At last I have found the book I need.

Stop the Bullying. A Handbook for Teachers by Ken Rigby will be enormously helpful for teachers, administrators, parents, students and others who care about establishing and maintaining safe environments for children to work and play in. The book provides many useful ideas for developing a well-defined anti-bullying policy, securing a healthy school ethos, and encouraging role models who are knowledgeable and caring and who are active in working towards solutions to the bullying problem.

Hope for Parents and Students

Ken Rigby sends very clear messages throughout the handbook. He is not afraid to tackle the layered aspects to the problem. He insists that we should be concerned with the quality of relationships that exist in the whole school community, that bullying should be taken seriously, and that there needs to be a joint resolve to deal with the difficulty. Mr. Rigby asks all adults and children to become more aware of the persistent problem and sensitive to the harm that bullying can do. He gives advice about how to work collaboratively to eliminate it. Often he tells us that bullies have low levels of empathy. Mr. Rigby also explains why people bully, how the personality, the social context and societal influences can foster conditions for bullying to happen. He also writes about why people do not bully. For me as an educator, this was very helpful information. Bullying does not happen in schools where students believe bullying is wrong, have high levels of empathy, feel successful, have a wide variety of social skills and are generally occupied with and are enjoying what they are doing in school.

Throughout the book, I was struck by how seriously Mr. Rigby takes this persistent problem and how convincing his arguments are. I think back to the drama classes that I conducted with the students in the anti-bullying project in the Toronto schools. I remember a student saying how she often felt overwhelmed by all that she was experiencing and that she just needed to know that the bullying that was happening to her would eventually stop. Ken Rigby's book provides hope for this student and others. He provides us with the facts, encourages us to acknowledge the problem and inspires us with a desire to "stop the bullying" so that the lives of children can change dramatically. As I continue my work in drama as an anti-bullying intervention, I will rely upon the information in this book to help me. Because of it, I have enormous hope that there will come a day as Ken Rigby says, "when bullying simply doesn't happen."

Kathy Lundy
August 2001

THE PURPOSE OF THE HANDBOOK

This handbook is to help us deal more effectively with the problem of bullying in schools. Those who educate about bullying include both teachers and parents. It is only through mutual understanding of each other's role and a joint resolve to work collaboratively with each other that the problem of bullying will ever be solved. Hence, although this handbook is directed primarily at informing educators, I hope that it will also be read by parents who care about bullying in schools, who want to know what can be done about it, and who want to work closely with schools to help stop the bullying.

Since the 1970s there has been increasing attention paid to the problem throughout the world. In a major book on the subject published in 1999 titled The Nature of Bullying (edited by Peter Smith and others), there are accounts by researchers in 34 countries and from every continent of bullying in schools. Research on issues in school bullying continues to be published in journals at an increasing rate. International and national conferences are now examining bullying as a central theme. It is not easy to keep up with this flow of information.

At the same time, the issue of school bullying is a growing community concern. This is reflected in the importance that is being attached to the issue in the media. It is also evident in encouragement that is sometimes given to parents to take legal action against a school when they believe there has been a breach in the duty of care that schools have in protecting children from severe forms of peer bullying. This may sometimes create a doomsday illusion that bullying is becoming ever more prevalent in an increasingly dysfunctional society. This is not the case. What is happening is that we are becoming more sensitive to the harm bullying can do, less into denial that it is happening, and generally more optimistic that bullying can be greatly reduced.

For several years now some progressive schools have been taking the matter very seriously and are putting in place excellent policies and programs against bullying. Quite recently some Education Departments have begun to respond, as they should, by insisting that all schools have policies and procedures for dealing with bullying. Resources are becoming available to help schools with the task of educating and training school staff to respond effectively.

The purpose of this handbook is to provide educators with a set of basic facts, ideas and suggested procedures in a convenient format to help eliminate the manifest evil of bullying in schools.

I am encouraged to try my hand at this because over the last 12 years I have kept abreast of bullying research and contributed substantially to it through more than 30 books and papers in international academic research journals. Such research is not very accessible to the general reader, and indeed has needed to be translated, as it were, from the academic jargon into sound practical advice. Although running a school and getting the best out of everyone are skills that normally develop through personal experience and are honed by practice, I believe we can learn from research and benefit from the experience of those who have wrestled with the persistent problem of bullying in schools.

While the main focus of this handbook is on bullying among students, we need to spread the net wider to include the whole school community. It is obvious that bullying and harassment often occur between adults in the workplace. In fact the second wave of research into bullying has centred exclusively on workplace issues. In some schools, teachers have claimed that they are being bullied by their peers, sometimes by students, and occasionally by the parents of students.

For their part, students sometimes claim that they are bullied by their teachers. Parents may also believe that teachers have bullied them when they have sought help for their children. Not only are such encounters distressing, but also they provide models of inappropriate behaviour that can positively encourage bullying behaviour among students. Therefore it is important that in addressing the problem of bullying in schools we should be concerned with the quality of relationships that exist in the whole school community. We need to take this wider perspective.

To round out this discussion, I have included a number of activities for educators, students and parents alike to enable them to confront and work through their experiences more effectively. These useful tools, located at the end of the book, take the form of questionnaires, warning signs, quizzes and alternative approaches to dealing with bullies. Through the promotion of greater understanding of bullying, as well as the presentation of some helpful actions and activities to counter it, I hope that this resource book will offer some hope and inspiration to "stop the bullying".

USING THE HANDBOOK

This handbook is designed primarily for people concerned with the social education of young people, whether as teachers or as parents.

The following are suggestions as to how the handbook may be used.

For school educators

1. First, appoint a coordinator for the development of an anti-bullying policy for the school. This person would work with a small number of other staff members to form the Coordinating Committee.

2. Each committee member would then meet with a group of staff to discuss the content of the handbook. Thus all staff members become involved. There can be, if required, several meetings at which the content of the handbook is discussed. Information from the Appendix can be used to provide overhead transparencies or handouts.

3. At group meetings, members should identify ideas and suggestions useful and applicable to their school.

4. At the end of the series of meetings, group leaders should share views expressed by their groups, and decide on what recommedations to make to the school. At this stage, the Committee may decide to coopt parent and/or student representation.

5. The Coordinating Committee should then prepare a document for distribution to each staff member outlining proposed actions to counter and reduce bullying.

6. This document may then be discussed at a general staff meeting and provide a basis for the school's anti-bullying policy.

For parents

1. Read the handbook with a view to understanding what ideas and suggestions are **now** being made by educators to reduce bullying.

2. After appraising what is suggested, you will be aware of options that are now available to schools. You will find this useful in understanding what schools and families can do to stop bullying and ensure that any approaches you might make to the school are informed.

3. The handbook can help parents who are considering educational alternatives and wish to choose the school that best provides for the safety of their children.

WHY BOTHER?

Occasionally – less and less often I am glad to say – you meet somebody who does not see, or does not want to see, what the fuss is about. You may hear these things said:

There may be a few schools around where nasty things like bullying and violence occur, but I'm glad to say that nothing like that happens at my school.

Sure kids do bully each other. So what! It helps to toughen them up. Shouldn't wrap them in cotton wool, anyway. No real harm is done.

There has always been bullying. There will always be bullying. Just human nature. No point in wasting your time trying to stop it.

We now know that **none** of these statements is true.

Hundreds of independent studies have been conducted in many countries, including Australia, to assess the incidence of bullying in all types of schools and there has never been a study in any school that has reported that bullying was not taking place.

Again, many studies have examined the question of whether children are affected adversely by being bullied and the answer is a unanimous "yes". We can list the areas:

1. **Lowered mental health:** damaged self-esteem; increased anxiety; deepened depression; increased likelihood of suicidal thinking; lowered level of happiness;

2. **Induced social maladjustment:** fear of other children; absenteeism from school; and

3. **Physical un-wellness:** rise in medical ill-health symptoms.

What is of particular concern is that serious and sustained bullying in schools can have devastating long-term effects on the health and wellbeing of people when they reach adult years. We should recognise too that although most victims are subdued, some become alienated and bitter, plot revenge and can be extremely dangerous to others.

Finally there **are** grounds for optimism. Studies show that there are large variations between schools in the prevalence of peer victimisation, and these cannot be accounted for in terms of background characteristics of students and their families. More crucially, interventions to reduce bullying have been shown to work.

Understanding Bullying

WHAT IS BULLYING?

How you define and describe bullying is of great practical importance because it determines what you focus on and ultimately what you do about it.

You need to be clear what it is and what it is not. To do justice to what bullying is, you need to recognise that:

1. **It begins when somebody (or a group of persons) wants to hurt someone or put that person under pressure.**

   Such a desire is a necessary but not sufficient condition for bullying to occur. Remember that a desire to hurt or pressure somebody may not be expressed in hurtful action, in which case bullying may not take place.

2. **Bullying involves a desire to hurt + hurtful action.**

   There may be actions of different kinds: physical or verbal or gestural, direct or indirect, or commonly a combination of these. But, in addition, there is an imbalance of power, at least in the situation in which the bullying takes place.

3. **Bullying involves a desire to hurt + hurtful action + a power imbalance.**

   Although you may reasonably want to stop it, fighting or quarrelling between people of equal strength or power is not bullying. But in addition, bullying is conceived as behaviour that is not just.

4. **Bullying involves a desire to hurt + hurtful action + a power imbalance + an unjust use of power.**

   Hence we must always ask whether the hurtful use of superior power is justified or not (see Section 7). In addition, bullying actions are typically repeated.

5. **Bullying involves a desire to hurt + hurtful action + a power imbalance + an unjust use of power + (typically) repetition.**

   It is characteristic of bullying that the perpetrator enjoys the domination that is being demonstrated and the victim feels oppressed.

> **Bullying involves a desire to hurt + hurtful action + a power imbalance + (typically) repetition + an unjust use of power + evident enjoyment by the aggressor and a sense of being oppressed on the part of the victim.**

GENDER, RACE, DISABILITY AND SOCIAL CLASS

Over the last 10 years or so, there has been a lot said and written about bullying and harassment occurring as a consequence of prejudiced thinking and discrimination, more especially on the basis of gender, race and disability. Education Departments have understandably emphasised the importance of these factors.

1. **Gender:** How individuals define "masculinity" and "femininity" can have a significant effect on how they treat others. For example, when a boy sees himself as very tough, aggressive or macho, he is prone to despise and harass other boys who are gentle and artistic. Similarly, a girl who sees herself as "feminine" in the conventional sense may look down on other girls who are rough, "unladylike" or "butch". This line of thinking does indeed explain some bullying behaviour, for instance that of boys who deride and seek to upset those they see as "gay". Sex-based harassment has been identified as occurring frequently among Australian schoolchildren.

   Most bullying goes on within gender groups. Generally, physical bullying goes on mainly between boys and relational bullying goes on mainly between girls. Verbal bullying, however, is not uncommon between genders, with girls being subjected much more to disparaging and hurtful remarks from boys than vice-versa. The problem of changing the attitudes and verbal behaviour of boys towards girls in schools – and its continuation in later years – is a particularly pressing one.

2. **Race:** Although the term is now seen as having little scientific credibility and is consequently avoided in favour of "ethnicity", there can be no doubt that feelings of superiority because one belongs to a particular ethnic group, usually a socially dominant group, can give rise to bullying and harassment. At the same time, research has shown that racial or ethnic group differences need not render one group more susceptible to being bullied than another.

3. **Disability:** Bullying is sometimes directed towards children who do not have the same physical or mental capabilities as others, for example children who are diagnosed as ADD or have speech defects.

4. **Social class:** Where there is a mix of children from families of high and low socioeconomic status, some being rich and others poor or unemployed, the possibility of bullying, especially through social exclusion, must always be present. However, research does not consistently support the view that, in a school, children from families of low socioeconomic status are victimised more than others.

Explanations that relate to the above factors can account for a good deal of bullying and harassment, and useful instructive material has become available to schools in recent years. However, not all bullying can be explained in this way. We should bear in mind that there are many examples of schools in which differences in social class and ethnicity do not inevitably give rise to children bullying each other.

POWER INEQUALITIES

Differences in power between individuals and between groups make bullying possible.

Power may be defined generally as the capacity to produce an intended effect. It may be used or abused.

In schools there are large differences in power that can be employed to bully others. This is partly due to the fact that schools cater to children of different ages and maturity, and personal and social characteristics. Further, the element of compulsion in school education implies that the staff in a school must have the power to act authoritatively in dealing with students. Added to this, the hierarchical structure in school organisations results in some staff members having a higher degree of institutional or legitimate power than others.

We can identify a number of specific sources of power that some members of a school community enjoy:

1. **The capacity to dominate others physically:** This may be related to size, strength and fighting skills. This is likely to be more important among boys, especially in elementary schools when physical encounters are more common.

2. **Sharpness of tongue:** Related to verbal skills, especially quickness of wit. As children become older, these qualities become more potent means of bullying others.

3. **Ability to call on others for support:** Related to popularity, social skills and the capacity to manipulate others. This applies especially to so-called "relational bullying".

4. **Status in a group:** Related to having valued accomplishments, such as sporting ability, being personally attractive, being a member of a majority, mainstream group as opposed, for example, to being in an ethnic minority, disabled or not heterosexual.

5. **Institutionalised or ascribed authority:** Related to position in an organisation, for example principal, teacher or student, prefect and, in some schools, senior as opposed to junior.

Bear in mind that power is not fixed. A person may acquire or lose power. For example, a child may learn to become more assertive; a teacher may lose the capacity to control a class. Power is fluid.

Note also that power is often situation-bound; for example, the capacity to dominate physically may be a means of bullying in the schoolyard, but not in a well-run classroom.

WHEN FORCEFULNESS IS NOT BULLYING

It should not be assumed that when a more powerful person acts forcefully in a given situation and places someone under some pressure that he or she is necessarily engaging in bullying. It is acknowledged that persons in authority should have some powers to insist on appropriate behaviour within certain defined areas.

The use of teacher authority with students

Under some circumstances, teachers are currently empowered to employ verbal reprimands, exclude children from classes or selected activities, and order detentions. On the other hand, the use of physical force (hitting or caning), the continual use of sarcasm at a child's expense, and repeated shouting at or threatening children are regarded as unjustified and can be described as "bullying".

The line between the forceful use of teacher authority and bullying is sometimes not easy to draw. Indeed, in recent years the "correct" line has repeatedly shifted.

The use of authority consistent with assigned non-teaching role

The role may fit into a school hierarchy, as in principal, deputy principal, and other staff, and entail power to direct others. In addition, some roles may have a specialised non-hierarchical function, as in the case of the year coordinator, librarian, and school secretary. Each has a degree of authority that may be appropriately applied. For example, a principal may allocate staff duties; a librarian may insist on a quiet atmosphere in the library. Bullying occurs when such authority is misapplied or used excessively.

Roles may also be assigned among students, as occurs when class leaders or school captains are elected or appointed. Again, bullying can occur when such leaders act in ways that are not consistent with role requirements. This is evident in schools where senior students are empowered to discipline junior students and sometimes engage in victimisation. This can happen to a greater degree in boarding schools.

Degree of provocation

Sometimes when force is used by a more powerful person, it is in response to provocation by an individual or group; for example, when junior students set out to tease older students or when teachers are targeted and class work is disrupted by mischievous students. Although the circumstances may not fully justify a forceful reaction, they may reduce the culpability of the actions and should be judged accordingly.

We may conclude that although in most cases it is not difficult to recognise what is bullying, there are certainly grey areas. What should be done in these circumstances must be continually debated.

THE MEANS OF BULLYING

The ways people bully can be classified (with examples) as follows.

	DIRECT	**INDIRECT**
Verbal abuse	• Verbal insults • Unfair criticism • Name calling	• Persuading another person to criticise or insult someone • Spreading malicious rumours • Anonymous phone calls and e-mails
Gestural abuse	• Threatening or obscene gestures • Menacing stares	• Deliberate turning away or averting one's gaze to ignore someone
Physical means	• Striking • Throwing things • Using a weapon • Removing or hiding belongings	• Getting another person to assault someone
Relational bullying	• Forming coalitions against someone	• Persuading people to exclude someone

For all groups of persons – students, teachers and parents – **verbal means** are the most common form of bullying. The means may vary in sophistication or subtlety, from crude name-calling and up-front insults more common among children, to the use of cruel sarcasm, innuendo and rational-sounding (but knowingly unfair) criticism employed by older students and adults. **Indirect verbal bullying** may occur when the perpetrator seeks to hurt someone without revealing his or her identity. **Gestural bullying,** again, may vary in subtlety from finger signs and tongue poking to rolling of the eyes and a deliberately inappropriate poker face. In most school communities, **physical means** are the least commonly practised, but occur more frequently among boys and among younger students. Although not physically hurtful, the continual removing of belongings is common in many schools. The effectiveness of **relational bullying** depends on deliberately reducing the enjoyment a victim may have through satisfying personal relationships, and appears to be practised more among girls.

A further distinction is between bullying perpetrated by **individuals** and bullying by **groups**. The distinction is sometimes difficult to make because individual bullies are often sustained by groups or associates. But some bullying is exclusively one to one, while another type may consist of group against an individual who may be a student, a teacher or a parent.

In practice, bullying may involve several or all of these means, but remember that it is not just the actions themselves that constitute bullying. One must also take into account the power imbalance and whether the actions were justified or not.

9 SEXUAL HARASSMENT

Sexual harassment is akin to bullying and should be included when a school considers what it can do to stop bullying. It may be defined as unwelcome conduct targeting the gender of another person that may reasonably be judged as offensive, humiliating or intimidating. Therefore, while the first and essential criterion is whether the conduct of the perpetrator is unwelcome, a further consideration is the judgment of a fully informed and reasonable person.

Broadly speaking, sexual harassment implies that a person is being put under unacceptable pressure in the area of their sexuality, and accordingly feels oppressed. The perpetrator or perpetrators, as in bullying, are abusing their power.

We should bear in mind that sexual harassment can and does take place from time to time between people of the same gender, as well as between males and females. It can happen between schoolchildren of all ages, between staff members and between staff and students.

As in bullying, we recognise different means by which sexual harassment is carried out. These can include:

1. **Physical means:** as in unwanted contact of a sexual nature, for example touching breasts or genitalia.

2. **Verbal:** as in unwanted comments, which may be spoken or written, drawing attention to a person's actual or alleged sexual characteristics or sexual orientation, such as having big, small or "no" breasts; being heterosexual, homosexual or "non-sexual". Comments or written messages, for example by e-mail, may suggest that a person lacks an acceptable sexual identity, being, for example, "cold", "frigid" or "butch".

3. **Gestural:** as in offensive finger gestures, cynically thrown "kisses" or deliberate staring intended to embarrass.

4. **Indirect:** as in spreading rumours orally or through graffiti about someone's sexual activities or orientation and seeking to have others treat that person deprecatingly because of their sexuality.

The motivation behind sexual harassment is commonly to hurt in some way, which is invariably the case with bullying. But one must bear in mind that in some cases what is experienced by the victim as sexual harassment is a crude and socially unacceptable attempt to gain sexual satisfaction, or even to initiate or advance a sexual relationship with someone. Hence, there is sometimes a need to distinguish between sexual harassment and bullying.

BULLYING AS A DYNAMIC PROCESS

It is useful to see bullying as a process that typically persists over time with outcomes depending on a number of definable factors. To understand how bullying begins, start with a scenario in which someone is seen as a potential victim of systematic aggressive behaviour. Anybody may fit this category, but it is more likely that the potential victim will display characteristics that suggest weakness and vulnerability. Bullying is deliberate. Plans are made to put the targeted person under pressure, typically to hurt, undermine and humiliate. Different kinds of action follow and the cycle begins, sometimes with other people joining in to maintain the bullying.

BULLYING CYCLE BEGINS

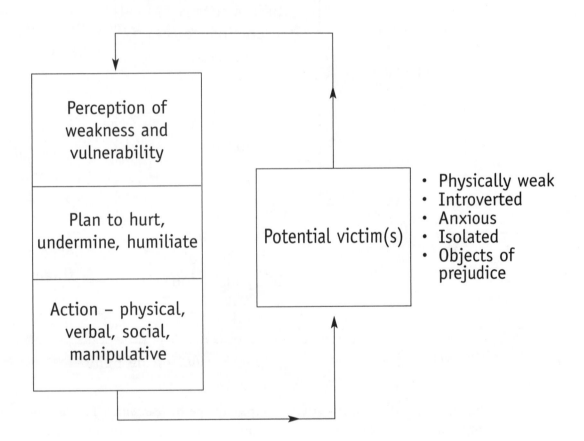

 **THE PASSIVE VICTIM**

Some victims may be called passive victims as they do not resist. The following diagram shows what typically happens.

BULLYING AND THE PASSIVE VICTIM

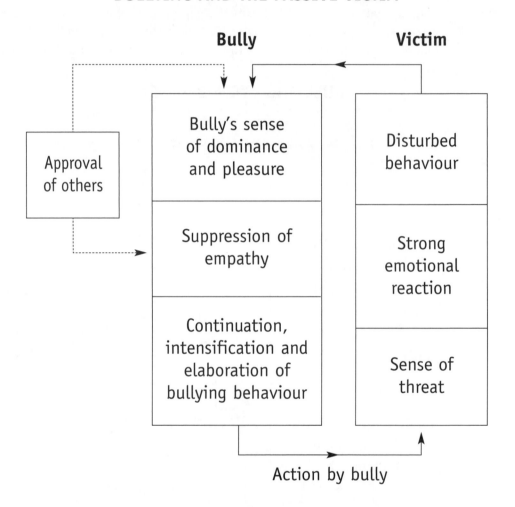

The reaction of the passive victim is typically one of fear, either because the threat is overwhelming or because of a fearful disposition, or both. The victim may be petrified.

He or she may see no way of responding effectively. During the bullying, the victim may appear zombie-like or alternatively wildly emotional. Subsequently, the victim is likely to appear upset and depressed.

The victim's reaction may reinforce the bully's or bullies' behaviour. They have achieved the intended effect. If there is approval from others – especially from bystanders when the bullying occurs – the sense of dominance and pleasure may increase. The chances of an empathic reaction to the victim's distress are lessened. The bullying is likely to continue. It may become more elaborate as new ways of bullying the victim are discovered. It may become more intense. As long as the bullying gives satsfaction and there is no intervention, the cycle continues. We know that such cycles can continue unabated for many weeks, months, even years.

THE RESISTANT VICTIM

With the resistant victim, a different story may unfold. In this case, the victim may see the bullying behaviour as a challenge rather than a foregone conclusion and make plans to counter it in some way. The diagram suggests different possibilities.

BULLYING AND THE RESISTANT VICTIM

Bully		Victim

```
                    Challenge to              Escapes  Fights back  Acts cool  Seeks help  Distracts
                    bully's dominance

                    Bully re-appraises plan

         Bully      Bully      Devises       Plan to counter the bullying
         desists    contin-    new
                    ues        ways          Perceived challenge

                                             Sense of threat
```

Bullying stops   Bullying continues

The victim may seek to employ one or more of the following ways of coping:

1. **Escapes:** The victim may find ways of escaping from the bullying situation and may minimize chances of encountering the bully/bullies on future occasions.

2. **Fights back:** Fighting back, physically or verbally, may be an option. In some circumstances, a student may overcome the problem by taking appropriate physical training or (less dangerously) learning how to react more assertively.

3. **Acts cool:** Appearing unperturbed, acting nonchalant, may sometimes be the best way to respond, especially with low level teasing or name-calling.

4. **Seeks help:** Help may be sought from various quarters; from other students, parents, and school authorities. Many students are unwilling to seek help because "dobbing" is unacceptable by peers or because it may make matters worse.

5. **Distracts:** Distracting, amusing or placating a bully so that he or she begins to behave more positively is a possible strategy.

Under some circumstances, each of these strategies may be effective in lessening or countering the bullying. However, these strategies are often unsuccssful and the bullying continues.

BULLYING INVOLVING SCHOOL STAFF

Bullying in schools can also involve staff in several ways.

1. **The bullying of students by staff.** This can sometimes happen under these circumstances:
   a. Unrealistic goals are being set and insisted upon for individual or group performance of students.
   b. Methods of putting pressure on students to perform are unacceptable, e.g., through the use of threats and excessive punishment for failure, and especially the use of sarcasm and public humiliation for non-achievement.
   c. An attempt to gain or maintain "control" over a class involves singling out individuals repeatedly for disciplinary action, without clear justification.
   d. The teacher is motivated by personal prejudice to discriminate against students with characteristics over which they have little or no control, e.g., personal appearance, way of speaking, social background, or gender identification.

Remember, as a teacher, one has an obligation to motivate children to reach high standards and also to maintain order in classrooms. Students sometimes see that bullying by a teacher is in fact an appropriate approach to discipline; but real cases of teacher bullying do happen, are damaging to students and provide a model for students who would bully others.

2. **The bullying of teachers by students.** This can and sometimes does happen, especially under these circumstances:
   a. Inadequate classroom management skills — which teachers need to improve.
   b. Teaching to an inappropriate curriculum or using an inappropriate teaching style, resulting in students becoming frustrated and/or bored.
   c. When a group of students deliberately sets out to torment or upset a teacher.

Teachers who are being consistently bullied by students may need to improve their teaching and managing skills and should receive help and support from colleagues to do so. At the same time, when students do bully staff, decisive action must be taken by school authorities to stop it.

3. **Bullying between adults in the school community.** This includes bullying that occurs between colleagues in a school and between parents and staff. This may occur when:
   a. People in authority in a school seek to exercise control outside their role requirements (these should continually be clarified).
   b. Personal antagonisms result in one person systematically seeking to dominate and/or humiliate another.
   c. Teachers and parents fail to recognize their obligations: that teachers have a duty of care and parents have responsibilities to work constructively with schools. Bullying may arise when each is insensitive to the difficulties experienced by the other in addressing a complex situation in which a particular child has serious problems at school.

Although the major concern in schools is bullying among students, bullying involving adults in the school community greatly adds to the problem of peer victimisation, and this too must be addressed in every school.

WHY SOME PEOPLE BULLY

As we have seen, the existence of power imbalances in a school community make bullying possible. Of course, not all people make use of their greater power to bully someone. Here are suggestions as to why some do.

1. **They think that bullying pays;** in some schools they are admired by others; they are able to get what they want; and they are less likely than others to be victimised.

2. **They are aggressive and impulsive,** which makes them constitutionally more inclined to engage in bullying.

3. **They enjoy the submission of others.**

4. **Bullying others is consistent with a macho or imposing image** a person may have, especially if one is male but increasingly so for females.

5. **It seems like fun,** especially when one is part of a group engaged in teasing someone.

6. **They have relatively low levels of empathy,** which results in a bully being unaffected by the evident distress of others.

7. **Prejudice leads them to believe that some kinds of people deserve to be bullied;** for example, people of a different ethnic group or of a different sexual orientation.

8. **A generalised hostility towards others** has been engendered by negative experiences with parents and families, especially feeling unloved and/or over-controlled.

9. **They have been influenced by aggressive "models",** in real life and/or by viewing violent videos.

10. **The victim is perceived as having provoked the negative treatment;** commonly bullies see their bullying behaviour as "pay-backs".

11. **Chronic boredom at school** may result in bullying as a means of making life more interesting.

12. **The achievement of desired goals** is seen as more important than the insensitive means employed to attain them. This applies particularly to some people in management positions.

13. **They are slaves to authority,** prepared unquestioningly to do their bosses' "dirty work" by imposing on others.

14. **They see it as part of their role;** for example, as a prefect or teacher.

Some of these proposed explanations for bullying behaviour relate to personality, others to the social context or to social and societal influences. Each may contribute.

WHY SOME PEOPLE DO NOT BULLY

Since a primary aim in countering bullying is to prevent it from happening at all, it is sensible to ask the question: Why is it that some students do not bully, or do so very rarely?

The most obvious reason might be because in general they can't, being less powerful than other students. This is true of some. However, there are numerous cases of students who believe they are more able than others to bully their peers if they wanted to, but do not do so. They do not bully because:

1. **They feel that bullying is wrong.** Substantial numbers of students report that they "would feel ashamed of themselves" if they bullied someone.

2. **They have a high level of empathy** and dislike to see people suffer.

3. **They have social skills** that enable them to get what they want without resorting to bullying.

4. **They are generally so occupied** and enjoying what they are doing, so that bullying someone doesn't occur to them or is uninteresting.

5. **They feel they are successful** in what they do at school and are not inclined to displace anger or frustration by bullying others.

6. **They see the role they fill as being inconsistent with undermining others;** for example, as a prefect, football captain, peer support member or even a "good student".

7. **They have been exposed repeatedly to positive modelling** by influential peers or adults.

8. **They believe that bullying others doesn't pay.** This may be because they believe that negative consequences will follow if they do engage in acts of bullying (for instance, they believe that school authorities will find out and impose sanctions); and their bullying will be deplored (not admired) by those who matter to them (friends, parents, and possibly teachers).

9. **They have enjoyed positive experiences in the home** and generally feel positive towards others.

10. **They have internalised moral principles** that are incompatible with bullying.

11. **They feel obliged to accept the rules of the school** which indicate that bullying behaviour is not acceptable.

Action to Counter Bullying

SETTING GOALS

It is sensible to begin by setting out what you hope to achieve through an anti-bullying program for your school.

Here are my suggestions:

> **The general aim of the program is to make the school a safer, happier place for everyone.**

Progress in achieving this goal is indicated by:

1. A reduction in the number of persons who are victimised by others.

2. A reduction in the severity of victimisation.

3. A reduction in the number of people who engage in bullying others.

4. An increase in the support that is provided to those who are victimised in any way.

You need to consider ways in which progress towards these goals can be assessed. The following are some suggestions:

1. Make use of anonymous questionnaires from which reliable and relevant self-report data can be obtained. (Section 20 describes available questionnaire resources.)

2. Make assessments before the anti-bullying program is put into effect and again some time afterwards. Allow at least a one-year interval between testing. Remember that a program may actually raise awareness of what constitutes bullying, and that if there is a significant reduction in reported victimisation, this probably underestimates the actual reduction.

3. In your analysis of the data, identify precisely where and in what ways changes have occurred, for example according to year and gender, and in relation to both behaviour and attitudes. You may also wish to assess whether there have been changes in behaviour and attitudes towards specific groups, such as ethnic minorities.

4. Gauge whether the help provided to victimised students has really been effective in helping them to cope.

5. One focus should be on how students who have engaged in repeated bullying have changed (if at all) as a result of school disciplinary activities and/or counselling.

6. Gather supplementary data based on judgments from students and teachers who were present at school before and after the intervention.

7. Because a program may have many elements, it is useful to identify which elements were responsible for any change.

MAKING A PLAN

Here is a plan that may be adopted (or adapted) to reduce bullying in one's school.

1. **Educate the school community about bullying.** This is a necessary first step and implies both an understanding of the phenomena of bullying and a knowledge of what can be done to reduce its occurrence. The educational process should include in different ways and to a different extent the school staff, students and parents.

2. **Find out what is happening among members of the school community that is relevant to bullying.** You need to understand the nature and scope of the problem before it can be effectively addressed.

3. **Develop an appropriate and well supported anti-bullying policy.** This should be based on the school's understanding of bullying, and especially on what has been discovered about bullying at your school. It should provide a guide as to what is to be done.

4. **Establish what staff can do in their everyday work to reduce bullying and support students who are being victimised at school.** What can be done should be communicated to all staff members and serve as a guide and reminder of how they can help ease the problem.

5. **Ensure that teachers talk with students about bullying.** Provide guidance to teachers on how this can be done in such a way as to discourage bullying and gain student cooperation in countering peer victimisation.

6. **Empower students.** Create opportunities and provide necessary support or training for students to play a positive role in countering bullying and improving peer relations in the school.

7. **Devise procedures for dealing appropriately with incidents of bullying.** Alternative approaches need to be considered and evaluated, and distinctions made according to the nature and severity of the bullying.

8. **Provide support for those who are victimised.** Guidelines are needed on the role staff may play in helping students involved in bully/victim problems and how help can best be provided.

9. **Work cooperatively with parents.** This includes setting out how parents can be included in plans to reduce bullying, and how the school can work most effectively with parents whose children become involved in problems at school as victims or as bullies.

EDUCATING THE SCHOOL COMMUNITY

An anti-bullying program cannot succeed if the school community is not educated about bullying. It is important to bear in mind that the school community includes the staff and students in a school as well as the parents of the students. Not all of them are well informed, which is not at all surprising because much of our knowledge about bullying and its effects is quite recent.

Fortunately, there are now many resources available in the form of books, videos, articles and websites. Some of the more useful books are listed on page 46. A school may decide to purchase the ones they think would be most helpful. Those that are of the greatest interest and relevance to students should be in the school library.

Students can be educated about bullying through the curriculum and through special meetings to discuss the issue of bullying (see Section 28).

Parents can be informed through newsletters and invited to attend meetings at the school. After they have answered a questionnaire about bullying — and a surprisingly large proportion are keen to do so — many will be ready to attend. An informed speaker is needed to address parent groups. An increasing number of people are making it their business to read the literature on bullying and can be called upon to help. In Toronto, for example, Professors Debra Pepler and Wendy Craig are among the world's greatest experts in this area. It is an excellent idea to present some information to the group about what has been already been discovered about the school from surveys. But perhaps the most important part of educating people about bullying is to facilitate the sharing of personal bullying experiences and discussion of ideas about how it can be countered. This is true of all groups that come together to talk about bullying, whether they are composed of teachers, students or parents.

Besides meetings to raise awareness and share ideas, it is good to organise workshops at which useful skills can be taught to teachers on how to deal with problems that arise when children bully others or are bullied themselves. These include:

- Working with bullies
- Helping victims to cope more effectively
- Practising and teaching mediation techniques to resolve conflict
- Gaining the support of students in classes to help counter bullying
- Working constructively with parents of bullies and victims
- Developing well-supported and sound anti-bullying policies

Some basic information about each of the above is presented in this book, but more knowledge can be acquired from other books, videos and experts that can readily be accessed. However, we need to keep in mind that little can be achieved without practice and the sharing of one's understanding with each other.

WHAT IS USEFUL TO KNOW ABOUT YOUR SCHOOL

It is useful to know the nature, extent and consequences of bullying in your school in order to:

1. Raise everyone's awareness of the problem to a common level;

2. Motivate everyone to do something to stop the bad things that are happening; and

3. Establish a base-line for subsequent evaluations.

In addition, I think it is useful to know what people (staff, students and parents) would like to see done to counter bullying. This can provide a basis for discussion and drawing up acceptable and well supported plans and procedures.

Answers to these questions have been found to be of particular interest to schools:

- What kinds of bullying occur, and how common is each kind?

- Where at school does bullying happen most frequently?

- What proportion of children are being bullied?

- To what extent are different forms of bullying occurring, for example physical, verbal or relational?

- In which years or classes is bullying experienced most often?

- Are boys and girls bullied in similar or different ways?

- What evidence is there of sexual harassment?

- Are some groups (for instance, ethnic minority groups) being victimised more than others?

- How do students react to being bullied? Do they fight back? Do they tell?

- How do students say they have been affected by bullying?

- What proportion of children have stayed away from school because of bullying?

- How effectively are victimised children being helped?

- Do students want to talk about bullying in a classroom discussion?

- Are students interested in helping to stop bullying? If so, what might they do?

- Do teachers and parents want the school to have an anti-bullying policy?

- How do teachers and parents think that cases of bullying should be dealt with?

In addition to these, consider other questions you may want to see answered – questions that may be of particular interest to your school.

HOW TO GET THE FACTS

Much can be gleaned from everyday observations of how students interact with each other in classrooms and playgrounds, how staff treat each other, and the quality of their interactions with students and with parents. However, given the diversity of impressions observers commonly receive, it is sensible to make use of **anonymous** questionnaires answered by all the parties: students, teachers and parents. **Examples of short questionnaires are given in the section under Classroom Resources,** but some schools may want to access longer questionnaires that provide more information for a school. There are several reliable, longer survey instruments that have been widely used in Australia and overseas (see http://www.education.unisa.edu.au/bullying/). They include the following:

The Peer Relations Questionnaire (the PRQ) devised by Ken Rigby and P.T. Slee (1993). This is a questionnaire for students. It has been used by more than 100 schools and has provided information about bullying in elementary and secondary schools from over 38,000 students. It is a comprehensive research instrument that takes approximately 30 minutes to administer. The results need to be analysed by computer.

The Peer Relations Assessment Questionnaire (the PRAQ) developed more recently by Ken Rigby in 1995, consists of three versions to be answered by students, teachers and parents respectively. It has also been used by over 100 schools, and is relatively short and normally takes not more than 15 minutes to answer. Tally and summarising sheets are provided to enable the school to summarise the results. It is strongly advised that every staff member takes part in reading a sample of what the respondents say. Opportunity is provided on the questionnaire for respondents to make statements as well as to tick optional answers. The PRAQ can help greatly in raising awareness of the nature of the problem and how it is viewed by students, parents and teachers.

The School Relations Assessment Package (the SRAP). This is a new computerised system accessed through the Internet and was designed by Ken Rigby and Alan Barnes (2000). Based in part on previous questionnaires but with added content, this resource is available to schools with appropriate computing facilities. On completion of the questionnaires, a summary of group results can be provided within minutes.

For additional information on the PRQ and PRAQ and manuals contact:

Dr. Barrington Thomas
P.O. Box 104
Point Lonsdale, Victoria
Australia 3225
phone 03 52582340
fax 08 52583878
email: profread@pipeline.com.au

21 FINDING OUT ABOUT BULLYING FROM YOUNG CHILDREN

With very young school children (under 8 years) and children in kindergarten, it is not possible to obtain reliable information about bullying with a *written* questionnaire. Other methods are needed.

Direct observation is one way of getting some useful information about bullying. In this manner, it is usually possible to identify children who often bully others directly in the playground by physical, and to a lesser extent, by verbal means. This of course takes time and observers need to be prepared to spend some breaks and lunchtimes carefully monitoring what is happening. One can usually notice that some children are much more likely to be pushed around and called names than others. **Indirect bullying,** for example deliberately excluding individuals, is often less easy to observe, although one may notice that some children are more often on their own during the breaks and seem to be unwanted. These children may well be the targets of bullying.

Another method is to **talk to children individually** and ask them about their friends and how they are treated by others. Some teachers have found it useful and acceptable to interview children about whom they see as often being picked on or seeking to hurt others. There is usually a high consensus about who are seen as the bullies and the victims.

Recently, a questionnaire has become available that is appropriate for young, largely pre-literate students. It consists mainly of drawings which children can look at and indicate which person is most like them in encounters at school with other children. Of course, young children still need help to answer it and the teacher should go through the questions carefully with them, making use of transparencies on an overhead projector. Examples of some of the drawings are given on page 49.

Answers to these and other questions can provide indications of the extent to which children in a class are conscious of being bullied or harassed in different ways, as well as the extent to which children actually see themselves engaging in such behaviours. The results enable staff to obtain a benchmark against which they can measure the success of policies and programs designed to reduce bullying behaviour.

See further details on obtaining copies of this and other questionnaires relevant to bullying on page 29.

DEVELOPING AN ANTI-BULLYING POLICY

Most schools now agree that they should have a specific anti-bullying policy. This is not the same thing as a school discipline policy or a behaviour management policy. It may relate to these, but it needs to take into account the unique features of school bullying as defined earlier, as well as the perceptions and judgments of members of the school community.

Its purpose is to articulate where the school stands on the issue of bullying and, in general terms, what the school intends to do about it. These steps are suggested:

1. Hold a meeting with the school staff at which there is a presentation of what has been discovered about bullying at the school from the results of the questionnaires that have been administered. Make sure that the results are succinctly presented and clearly pertinent. It is useful to have a summary of the most relevant results available to every staff member. As well as quantitative information, it is useful to make use of selected quotations from what respondents have written.

2. Make appropriate use of information provided by staff members and parents as well as from students.

3. Discuss the implications from the findings and highlight the need to have a whole-school well coordinated response to the problem.

4. Have the task of formulating a draft anti-bullying policy for the school delegated to a selected group (see Section 2, Using the Handbook, for suggestions on how the committee might proceed). This group should be empowered to coopt student and parent representatives.

5. Ensure that the draft policy is critically examined by all interested parties and, if necessary, revised accordingly. To be most effective, the policy must be widely supported by students, teachers and parents.

Bear in mind that an anti-bullying policy should be a response to a situation identified as occurring at a particular school and should reflect the views of that school community. At the same time, it can be helpful to examine and discuss policies that have been produced at other schools, and consider how relevant (or irrelevant) they are to one's own school.

WHAT GOES INTO THE POLICY

An anti-bullying policy is a generalised response to bullying. It should provide principles and guidelines, not detailed procedures to deal with every conceivable case. The school will, on occasion, need flexibility. Here are some suggestions about what such a policy may contain:

1. A strong statement of the school's stand against bullying.

2. A succinct definition of bullying, with illustrations (see Sections 4 and 7).

3. A declaration of the rights of individuals in the school community – students, teachers, other workers and parents – to be free of bullying and (if bullied) to be provided with help and support.

4. A statement of the responsibilities of members of the school community: to abstain personally from bullying others in any way; to actively discourage bullying when it occurs; and to give support to those who are victimised.

5. A general description of what the school will do to deal with incidents of bullying. For example, the severity and seriousness of the bullying will be assessed and appropriate action taken. This may include the use of counselling practices, the imposition of sanctions, interviews with parents and, in extreme cases, suspension from school.

6. An undertaking to evaluate the policy in the near and specified future.

If there are concerns about anything contained in the document, make sure that these are thoroughly examined and resolved. The policy should eventually be widely disseminated, so that everyone in the school community knows what it contains. If necessary, there should be versions for parents of non-English speaking background. Different versions of the policy may be seen as appropriate, for example:

1. A general policy document consisting of a series of short statements on how the school is responding to the issue of bullying.

2. A document for parents explaining what they can do if their child becomes involved in a victim/bully problem at school (see Section 34).

3. A document for students on their rights and responsibilities and what they can do if they are victimised or if they see someone else being victimised.

4. A document for school staff detailing practical steps they can take when cases of bullying come to their attention. Also, what they can do if they are bullied by anyone at school. This document can include agreed, relevant administrative procedures for dealing with problems and the names of individual staff members who may have been assigned specialised roles for dealing with cases of bullying.

WHAT TEACHERS CAN DO ABOUT BULLYING

1. HELPING TO CREATE A SOCIAL ETHOS IN WHICH BULLYING IS LESS LIKELY TO HAPPEN

(i) Personally modelling pro-social, respectful behaviour in interactions with students, parents and other staff.

(ii) Developing and maintaining good classroom management. As well, it is important to avoid unduly pressuring or bullying students. Sometimes teachers under stress go beyond being appropriately authoritative and descend into sarcasm and intimidation.

(iii) Ensuring as far as possible that the educational tasks and the way they are presented engage the interests of all students. Sometimes students bully out of boredom.

(iv) Where practicable, include tasks that require cooperation between class members for successful completion.

(v) Minimise situations in which students are unoccupied, unsupervised, and in close proximity to others whom they may not wish to be near, especially over extended periods. This can and often does occur when teachers are late for a class or are called away from a class, and when students are waiting for long periods for a canteen to open or for public transport to arrive or are in transit on long journeys by bus.

2. ACTIVELY DISCOURAGING BULLYING

(i) By being observant and responding appropriately when bullying occurs in classrooms or at recess, according to the nature and severity of the bullying (see Sections 30 and 31).

(ii) Where appropriate, informing other staff members of incidents and initiating procedures agreed upon by the school to deal with perpetrators.

3. PROVIDING SUPPORT AND ADVICE

(i) By being open to listen to students who believe that they are being victimised (and to their parents) if they wish to talk about it.

(ii) By offering advice or suggestions, when asked, or by providing access to specialised counselling help if needed (see Section 32).

4. EDUCATING ABOUT BULLYING

(i) By facilitating class discussions on bullying at school.

(ii) Where practicable, developing in students relevant skills in assertiveness, conflict resolution and peer mediation (see Section 29).

25 TALKING WITH STUDENTS IN CLASS ABOUT BULLYING

Getting the active cooperation of students is a vital part of countering bullying. This involves talking with students individually and in groups about bullying and how they can help to stop it. It is more easily done with elementary school children and older secondary school students. But in all years, many students are keen to talk about it and comparatively few are against doing so. Students nearly always dislike and despise bullies and can, with your help, assist greatly in developing and implementing school policy. Here are some suggestions for conducting class discussions:

1. **Be clear about what you want to achieve with the group.** For example:

    (i) Recognise what bullying is.

    (ii) Experience feelings of concern and empathy for victims.

    (iii) Make constructive suggestions about what can be done to stop bullying.

    (iv) Undertake to act in ways to discourage bullying.

2. **Work with the class using methods that are suitable for the age group and with which *you* are comfortable.** But avoid a threatening, authoritarian approach which will antagonise some and polarise attitudes in the group. Don't preach. It is better to treat the class members as a resource for dealing with the problem. Here are some ideas:

    (i) **Arouse interest in the topic of bullying by first viewing an interesting video or film on the subject,** reading a book, examining relevant newspaper reports, or conducting a role-play illustrating bullying, or by having students write an essay describing conflicts between students at school. A focused discussion of bullying can then follow, leading to an examination of what can be done about it and, possibly, resolutions agreed on by the class.

    (ii) **Present specific problems relating to bullying incidents;** for example, how bystanders can be motivated to help rather than hinder students who are being targeted as victims.

    (iii) **Invite those who are interested in doing something to stop bullying to form an anti-bullying committee,** run by an interested teacher who is prepared to listen to their ideas about what students can do to reduce bullying in their school (see Section 27).

In addition, discuss with other teachers ways in which classes can be motivated to help reduce bullying. Be prepared to share both successes and failures.

FOCUS ON BYSTANDERS

We now know that bystanders can play a very big part in determining whether bullying continues or stops. Most bullying goes on in the presence of other students who react in different ways:

- Some support the bully by encouragement
- Some support the target of the bullying
- Some simply stand and watch

As we saw in the diagram on Section 11, the bully or bullies thrive on support and feel that others admire what they are doing. If nobody objects to what they are doing, they feel quite justified and even proud of themselves. They are then unlikely to feel any sympathy for the person they are bullying. The bullying is therefore likely to be repeated whenever they meet their "victim" again, especially if there is an audience. The victim may become increasingly upset by what is happening, as indeed may some observers.

Many children who are watching would like to see the bullying stopped. Sometimes they are simply afraid of what might happen to them if they do object. Sometimes they feel that they are not sure what to do to stop it — and think that others in the group are more able to act. It is therefore useful to explore with children how they feel when they see bullying going on and what they can do to help to stop it — without being harmed themselves.

On page 54 is an exercise that teachers may like to try with students in a classroom situation. Afterwards it may be possible to engage them in constructive discussion and perhaps role-play situations in which bystanders react in different ways to the situations they observe.

27 ROLES FOR EMPOWERED STUDENTS

In recent years, there has been much attention given to the part that students can actively play in reducing bullying. There are some clear advantages in gaining their assistance. We should bear in mind:

1. Students are much more likely to go to other students for help than to go to teachers when they are bullied.

2. Students usually have a much better, more realistic understanding of the nature of the relationships students have with each other.

3. Students are usually around when bullying takes place, especially during school breaks, and to and from school; teachers are rarely present at these times.

4. Some students are strongly motivated to help resolve interpersonal conflicts and can demonstrate high level skills in mediation and conflict resolution.

5. Students can often provide much needed information on bully/victim problems. They can coordinate their activities with those of staff members to discourage bullying.

THE ANTI-BULLYING COMMITTEE

This concept has been successfully employed in a number of schools in Australia.

1. It is composed of students who have volunteered to work together under the leadership of a staff member to help reduce bullying in a school.

2. Ideally it has students from every year of school and, in coeducational schools, has an appropriate gender balance.

3. It may include students who in the past have engaged in bullying, provided they have clearly committed themselves to helping to stop bullying.

4. The role of the staff member leading the group is to provide a sounding board for student ideas on how bullying at school can be countered, to encourage constructive plans and to provide the link between school policies and student initiatives.

Some of the things students may do are given on the next page.

Note: If students are to take on special roles, these should be defined clearly and unambiguously so that students know the limits of their responsibilities. They must also be provided with suitable training and support (see Section 29).

WHAT STUDENTS CAN DO ABOUT BULLYING

These are suggestions to show how students can actively participate:

1. **Take part in the development of the school policy against bullying.** Student representatives can make useful contributions and help to evaluate suggestions.

2. **Speak up at school assemblies against bullying.** Students who take a stand against bullying are far more influential than staff members who may simply make speeches.

3. **Form a welcoming committee** for new students when they start school.

4. **Help in the development of an orientation package for new students.**

5. **Visit feeder schools to reassure students** who will be coming to their school that they can count on being helped if they encounter any troublesome students.

6. **Help in publicising anti-bullying policies** by designing posters and writing about bullying in school magazines.

7. **Make it known that they will help fellow students** who have problems related to bullying. Students may be informed about how particular student-helpers can be contacted.

8. **Give advice to students** on how they might handle conflict constructively, avoid being bullied and get help if needed.

9. **Look out for students** who are having problems in their relationships with others and offer them support.

10. **Provide staff with information** about ongoing bully/victim problems, for example, where problems may be arising, and which students are involved.

11. **Help directly in the resolution of bully/victim problems.** Depending on the readiness of the school to approve the involvement of students in counselling or dispute resolution roles, selected students may act to resolve bully/victim problems under the general supervision of a staff member. For such work, the school may decide to provide special training and access appropriate resources (see Section 29).

12. **Help monitor changes in student behaviour** as a consequence of anti-bullying initiatives.

PROVIDING FURTHER HELP

There are now abundant resources aimed at reducing conflict in schools. These are relevant to addressing bullying because they help to create a school environment in which people enjoy more constructive relationships and where they are able to settle disputes that may otherwise end up with one person bullying another. Schools may decide to access these resources as a means of producing a happier, more peaceable school in which bullying is much less likely to happen.

Peer support is one such resource. This concerns fostering the physical and mental well-being of young people through the help they can receive from other students who have been suitably trained. There is a two-stage process: a peer support organisation first trains the teachers in the required methodology; teachers then train the students. Sessions are timetabled for senior students to work with groups of junior students, addressing relevant social and personal issues and suggesting and discussing solutions to problems. Anti-bullying is one of the issues that receives attention.

Conflict resolution skills are the means by which disputes may be resolved without the use of force or through the compliance of the less powerful party. Drama and role playing have been used to develop insights and teach children methods relevant to resolving conflicts at school. If these skills are well taught, bullying resulting from unresolved disputes will become much less likely. Also students who acquire these skills become more adept at handling difficult interpersonal relations, including attempts at bullying them. They may also become better at helping others in such situations.

Mediation This focuses on how a third party can help people engaged in a dispute or conflict that they are unable to resolve. Teachers who wish to acquire relevant skills can often do so by enrolling in centres of tertiary education or by attending workshops where such methods are taught. How effectively they can employ such skills in resolving student conflicts including bully/victim problems depends in part on the extent to which students trust them to undertake this task.

In some areas, training is available from professionals who provide workshops and seminars for students and also for teachers who subsequently oversee and monitor the students' work. Generally, peer mediation practised by students does not extend to cases where serious cases of bullying occur (these normally require adult intervention), but mediation by students in other cases may help to promote a school ethos in which bullying cannot flourish. Whether senior students may (and should) be trained to deal with bully/victim cases is controversial. Schools may, however, wish to investigate the feasibility of students engaging in this work.

Schools deciding to employ resources and methods described above should first count the cost (in time and expense) and also understand that a strong, sustained commitment to the practices is needed if their use is to be effective. But they should bear in mind that a happier school environment where students can concentrate on their studies more effectively and achieve greater satisfaction and success may be well worth the effort.

BULLY/VICTIM CASES

No two cases are exactly the same but we can identify broad types of cases, and these can have implications for how you go about trying to solve them.

THE INDIVIDUAL BULLY

1. The bullying is occurring in an ongoing relationship or derives from a past relationship. It is sustained by an unresolved dispute between two people. You may decide that mediation could work.

2. The bully is picking on one victim after another. This is the serial bully. Action generally needs to be taken by the school authorities to ensure that such behaviour is monitored and negatively reinforced, and alternative pro-social behaviours encouraged.

3. A very dominant person in authority may seriously bully an entire group. Work is needed with such a person to examine alternative means of influencing others and, in extreme cases, removal from the situation where people are being harmed.

BULLYING BY GROUPS

1. The group may consist of a duo who strongly reinforce each other in their acts of bullying. They seek victims. Sometimes one is clearly the leader and the other the accomplice. The duo can sometimes be extremely dangerous and their activities must be taken very seriously.

2. The group may be composed of members of roughly equal power and have relatively high cohesiveness; sometimes they have a ringleader. They may enjoy tormenting individuals with little or no justification because of a shared pleasure in doing so. Sometimes the target of bullying by the class is the teacher.

3. The group may be non-cohesive and include virtually everyone in an organisation. The bullying behaviour is directed towards an "outsider" and may become automatic for everyone.

4. Sometimes dominant groups bully other groups. This can occur when groups differ in power and status, the more powerful "in-group" acting abusively towards another group or groups.

In cases of group bullying, it is often best to work with group members individually (as in the Method of Shared Concern on page 61). However, if the group is brought together to confront the problem, it is best to include a number of pro-social students who can influence the outcome (see the so-called "No Blame Approach" on page 61).

ASSESSING THE SEVERITY OF BULLYING

As well as the type of case, you need to take into account the severity of the bullying. It is unreasonable to treat thoughtless (though hurtful) teasing in the same way as continual physical assault. The following diagram suggests how bullying is generally distributed in a school.

SEVERITY OF BULLYING BEHAVIOUR

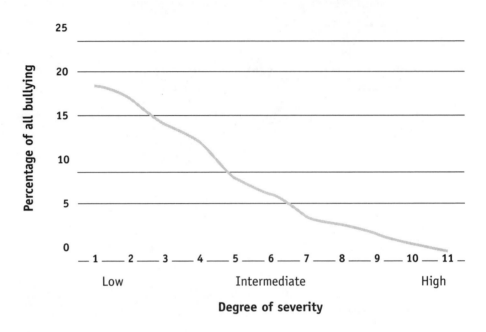

The figure shows the approximate distribution of bullying behaviour according to severity. To estimate severity, one would need to take into account:

(i) **the nature of the action,** for example mild teasing, which is generally not experienced as very hurtful, versus physical assault which is normally much more devastating;

(ii) **the frequency of bullying acts,** for example whether they occur daily, weekly or less often; and

(iii) **the duration of the bullying,** whether over a short or long time period.

For some purposes, for example in providing protection or support to victims, one may wish to take into account the vulnerability of the individual being targeted.

Low severity commonly involves thoughtless periodic teasing, name-calling and occasional exclusion. This can be annoying and unpleasant and can escalate and then involve more serious forms of bullying. Most bullying is at this level.

An intermediate level of bullying occurs when a child is subjected for a time to forms of harassment that are both systematic and hurtful. These may include cruel teasing, continual exclusion and some threats or some relatively mild physical abuse, for example pushing or tripping.

Severe bullying occurs when the harassment is cruel and intense, especially if it occurs over an extended period and is very distressing to the victim. It often involves serious physical assaults, but can still be severe when it is non-physical if the methods used are unremitting, occur over an extended period and are psychologically damaging.

HELPING THE VICTIMS

One of the responsibilities of members of a school community is that they should do what they can to help the victims of bullying. Here are some considerations that may affect **how** and **what** help might be given.

1. If a person has voluntarily come to you for help, it is most likely that you **can** help, if only by listening sympathetically. This is often all that the victim wants. We know that such help can be effective in reducing the negative impact bullying can have on a victim's physical or psychological wellbeing.

2. Be aware that on occasions the victim may be unwittingly provoking others and bringing on the bullying. This needs to be tactfully explored. Sometimes what the child needs is to develop skills of fitting in and making good friends.

3. When appropriate, offer practical advice on how the victim can learn to cope more effectively. Remember that if victims can solve the problem unaided, the rise in self-esteem is phenomenal. Assertiveness training is useful. But encouraging a victimised child to devise and deliver telling insults (a way of responding recommended by some anti-bullying gurus) can be, in many cases, to a child's disadvantage, especially if the child is being bullied by a stronger, physically aggressive person or by a group. In addition, such responding will certainly contribute to the general level of verbal abuse going on in a school.

4. It may be that the victim needs specialised help; for instance, he or she may be suffering from chronic anxiety, acute depression or from a post-traumatic stress disorder, in which case an appropriate referral should be made.

5. Upon close examination, it may be that intervention on the victim's behalf with the bully or bullies is needed. This is likely to be the case if the bullying is particularly severe or hurtful and action on the part of the victim is extremely unlikely to be effective; for instance, if a group of bullies is involved. In such cases, the victim's permission should normally be sought to initiate intervention with the bully or bullies in accordance with agreed upon school procedures.

6. In extreme cases, for example when very serious and health threatening bullying occurs, it may be decided that action must be taken without the victim's approval.

7. Make sure that records are kept of what has been done to help victimised children, and that the actions and outcomes are communicated, where appropriate, to interested parties, especially to parents.

HELPING THE BULLIES

Bullies need "help", not only because their behaviour is damaging to others, but also because of the harm that may be done to them as a consequence of them engaging in delinquent behaviour that brings them into conflict with the law.

Not all people who bully do so for the same reasons (see Section 14). Hence, individual bullies may be helped in different ways as described below:

1. Some individuals engage in bullying because they want somebody to do something for them and lack the necessary **social skills** to acquire what they want. They do not know how to act in such a way as to elicit positive reactions towards them or to gain another's cooperation. For a minority of students who bully, social skill programs are useful (see Section 15).

2. Often students who bully have had little or no experience of enjoying cooperating with others and sharing in the achievement of a common goal. So the provision of opportunities to engage in **cooperative learning** is important for them.

3. Students who bully sometimes have a strong need to lead or control others and they may be enabled to occupy roles which give them the opportunity to **exercise power in a socially desirable way**, for example in training or supervising other students in sporting activities. Students who have had a reputation for bullying others have sometimes reformed and taken a leading role in school anti-bullying committees. Care must be taken, however, that such power is not abused but exercised responsibly.

4. Where bullying is largely a result of inadequate **impulse control**, students can sometimes be helped through exercises promoting more thoughtful delayed responses. Socially desirable impulse control can be increased by systematic reinforcement of children's behaviour that is responsible and controlled.

5. Where bullying is a conforming response, seen as enjoyable because one is part of a group, change may sometimes be brought about through sessions with individual bullies who can be brought to act responsibly and discontinue bullying. **The Method of Shared Concern, by Anatol Pikas** is one way in which this may be achieved.

6. Family life sometimes engenders a tendency to bully others, either because family members model such behaviour or because home life is so frustrating that children wish to take it out on others. Through **interactions with parents**, school staff may have some (albeit limited) influence on how parents can best bring up their children.

7. Students who bully may change if they identify with powerful and – to them – attractive individuals who consistently act pro-socially. Hence by drawing attention to such **pro-social models**, a "bully" may come to act more like the person he or she admires. Often these are sporting heroes.

WORKING CONSTRUCTIVELY WITH PARENTS

School staff and parents may get together on bullying issues as a result of

(i) parents participating in the development of school policy;

(ii) parents expressing concern about their child's involvement in bully/victim problems, usually as a victim; or

(iii) the school requesting a meeting with parents of children who are bullying.

A basic right of parents is to speak with school staff if they believe their child is being bullied at school.

When the parents of victimised children meet with school staff, the following points are relevant:

1. Recognise that the parent is generally under a good deal of stress.

2. If a parent expresses anger directed at the school, remain understanding.

3. Make it understood that you do care and will do what you can.

4. Try to get the facts provided by the parent as clear as you can, but don't cross-examine or unduly emphasise inconsistencies in the parent's version of events.

5. Point out that you will need a little time (try to be specific) to investigate the matter yourself, but that you will certainly make contact again soon. There may be some circumstances, however, when a child's personal safety is severely threatened and action needs to be taken immediately.

6. Assure the parent of the existence of a school policy on bullying – if necessary, explain what it is – and the readiness of the school to take action against bullying.

7. Try to avoid getting into any argument, and above all don't set out to blame the parent, even if you suspect that the parent contributed to the problem.

8. Make it clear that you would be happy to see the parent again, if required.

With the parents of bullies:

1. Make sure that you already have as much reliable information about what has happened as you can.

2. Share your concern about what has been happening to the victim.

3. Avoid suggesting that it is the character of their child that is at fault. Rather emphasise that it is aspects of the behaviour of the perpetrator that must change. Try to refer to positive aspects of the child as well.

4. If it is decided that serious consequences for the perpetrator are to follow, for example suspension, point out that if there are no further episodes, the offence will no longer be part of his or her school record.

5. Be understanding, but firm.

Note: Except under special and justified circumstances, it is generally not helpful for the parents of bullies and victims to meet to solve the problem.

ADVICE FOR PARENTS

When parents discover that their child has been involved in bullying at school, either as a victim or as a bully, it can be very upsetting for them. They may feel at a loss. The school can provide advice to such parents along these lines:

1. If you suspect that your child is being bullied at school, encourage him or her to talk to you about it. Recognise that it may be hard for the child to speak out.

2. Never dismiss the matter by saying that it's the child's problem and he or she must simply stand up to the bully or bullies. Sometimes this course of action is impractical, especially if a group of bullies is involved.

3. Don't be too over-protective either, for example by saying: "Never mind. I will look after you. You don't have to go to school. Stay home with us."

4. Listen carefully and sympathetically. Try to get the relevant facts without interrogating the child.

5. Explore alternative courses of action with the child; for example, acting more assertively, making friends who can help, or speaking with a teacher or counsellor.

6. Decide whether it is best to discuss the problem with the school. This will normally depend upon: (i) the severity of the victimisation, including its duration; (ii) whether it is thought that the child can learn to cope; and (iii) the wishes of the child regarding whether the issue should be raised with the school. On occasions, if the bullying is particularly severe, you may reasonably ask the school for advice despite the reluctance of the child to seek such help.

7. If it is decided that the issue should be raised at school, be prepared to describe as accurately as possible what has been happening to your child.

8. Remember that the school needs to know what has been happening to your child for the good of all other children at the school. Also be aware that the school has a "duty of care" and is obliged to act "in loco parentis".

9. You should be assured that the case of bullying you describe will be carefully investigated and dealt with in accordance with the school's anti-bullying policy.

10. If you discover that your child is bullying others at school, take the matter very seriously and exercise whatever influence you can to stop this behaviour.

11. If the school informs you that your child has been bullying others and requests an interview, be prepared to work out a plan with the school to bring about a change in your child's bullying behaviour.

A CHECKLIST FOR SCHOOLS

This checklist enables you to make an assessment of how adequately your school has responded to the issue of bullying. Check how well it has done against each of the items below.

	Inadequately	Adequately	Outstandingly
1. Acquired useful resources for educating the school community about bullying			
2. Taken steps to gather facts about bullying at your school			
3. Developed school policy by involving: Staff Students Parents			
4. Produced an anti-bullying policy which: (i) Describes what bullying is (ii) Recognises the rights of individuals to be safe from being bullied (iii) Stresses the responsibility of everyone to help counter bullying (iv) Indicates in general terms how bullying incidents will be dealt with (v) Has the support of the school community			
5. Staff have discussed bullying with students			
6. Victimised students have been supported			
7. Incidents of bullying have been handled			
8. Students have been empowered to take part in action to counter bullying			
9. Students have acted to counter bullying			
10. Constructive meetings have been held with parents on issues of bullying			
11. Overall the school has been responding to bullying			
12. Plans made to review the anti-bullying work			

RESOURCES ON BULLYING IN SCHOOLS

BOOKS

Berne, S. (1996). *Bully-proof your child.* Melbourne: Lothian.

Bodine, R.J., Crawford, D.K., & Schrumpf, F. (1994). *Creating the peaceable school: A comprehensive program for teaching conflict resolution.* Champain, Illinois: Research Press.

Cowie, H., & Sharp, S. (1996). *Peer counselling in schools.* London: David Fulton.

Elliott, M. (1998). *Bullying.* London: Hodder Children's Books.

Farrington, D.P. (1993). *Understanding and preventing bullying.* In M. Tonny & N. Morris (Eds.). *Crime and justice.* (Vol. 17). Chicago: University of Chicago Press.

Garrity, C., Jens K., Porter W., Sager, N., & Short-Camilli, C. (1994). *Bully proofing your schools.* Opris West: Longmont, Colorado.

Johnson, D.W., & Johnson, R.T. (1991). *Teaching students to be peacemakers.* Edina, Minnesota: Interaction Book Company.

Juvonen, J., & Graham, S. (2001). *Peer harassment in school: The plight of the vulnerable and the victimized.* New York: Guilford.

Hazler, R.J. (1996). *Breaking the cycle of violence. Interventions for bullying and victimization.* London: Taylor & Francis.

Lewers, R., & Murphy, E. (2000). *The hidden hurt.* Ballarat: Wizard Books Pty Ltd.

Linke, P. (1998). *Let's stop the bullying.* Canberra: Australian Early Childhood Association.

Maines, B., & Robinson, G. (1992). *The no blame approach.* (The video). Bristol: Lame Duck Publishing.

Randall, P. (1996). *Bullying: A community approach.* Stoke on Trent: Trentham.

Ross, D.M. (1996). *Childhood bullying and teasing: what school personnel, other professionals and parents can do.* Alexandria, Va.: American Counselling Association.

Rigby, K. (1997). *Bullying in schools and what to do about it.* Markham, Ontario: Pembroke Publishers.

Rigby, K. (1997). *Manual for the peer relations questionnaire* (PRQ). Point Lonsdale, Victoria, Australia: The Professional Reading Guide.

Romain, T. (1997). *Bullies are a pain in the brain.* Raymond Terrace, NSW: Silvereye Educational Publications Pty Ltd.

Smith, P.K., & Sharp, S. (Eds.). (1994). *School bullying: insights and perspectives.* London: Routledge.

Smith, P.K., et al (Eds.). (1999). *The nature of school bullying.* London: Routledge.

Stones, R. (1993). *Don't pick on me.* Markham, Ontario: Pembroke Publishers.

Suckling, A. & Temple, C. (2001). *Bullying: a whole-school approach.* Melbourne: ACER.

Sullivan, K. (2000). *The anti-bullying handbook.* Oxford: Oxford University Press.

Classroom Resources

QUESTIONNAIRE FOR YOUNG CHILDREN

Here are some questions for you to answer. Your teacher will help you in understanding what you have to do. (Teachers: Please make overheads of the pictures to help to show how children can respond.)

Are you a boy or a girl? _____

How old are you? _____

What year of school are you now in? _____

Now look at these faces, which face is most like you when you are at school? (Circle the letter near the face most like yours?

Look at these 3 pictures. Then circle the letter (A, B or C) most like you at playtime?

Picture 1	Picture 2	Picture 3

Have you ever told a teacher that another student or students have tried to hurt you? (Circle "yes" or "no")

Have you ever tried to hurt another person at school who was not as strong as you are?

Yes, lots of times   Sometimes   Never

What is the nicest thing about your school?

_____

_____

_____

QUESTIONNAIRE FOR OLDER STUDENTS

Please answer these questions about your life at school. There is no need to give your name.

Year of class _____   Your age in years _____   Your sex _____

1. How well do you get on with students at this school? (Circle one of the following)

| Always well | Usually well | Well about half the time | Usually not well | Never well |

We are interested in what **bullying** goes on in this school. We call it bullying when people deliberately and repeatedly threaten or hurt a less powerful person by what they do or say.

2. Have you ever been bullied by another student or group this year? (Circle one)

Yes   No

3. If you have answered "yes", indicate how often each of the following has happened to you this year (Circle "never", "sometimes", or "often" in each case)

I have been hit or threatened	Never	Sometimes	Often
I have been called unpleasant names	Never	Sometimes	Often
I have been deliberately left out of things by others	Never	Sometimes	Often

4. How have you felt about being bullied by others? (Circle one answer)

| I was never bullied by anyone | I was bullied but not bothered by it | I was bothered a bit by it | I was upset a good deal |

5. Do you personally feel safe from being bullied at this school? (Circle your answer)

| Always | Usually | Half the time | Usually feel unsafe | Never feel safe |

6. Could you use some help to stop the bullying? (Circle your answer)

Yes   Unsure   No

Thank you very much

QUESTIONNAIRE FOR STAFF ON SCHOOL-PEER RELATIONS

This is a brief questionnaire for which no personal details are required. The focus is on **bullying** which can be described as occurring when people deliberately and repeatedly threaten or hurt a less powerful person by what they do or say.

1. What is your judgment of the extent of bullying at **this** school between students in the following way? (Circle your answer)

Students are bullied by being hit or threatened by others	Never	Sometimes	Often
Students are bullied by being called unpleasant names	Never	Sometimes	Often
Students are being bulied by being deliberately left out of things by others	Never	Sometimes	Often

2. How **safe** do you think children feel at this school from being bullied by other students? (Circle your answer)

Always feel safe	Usually feel safe	Half the time feel safe	Usually feel unsafe	Never feel safe

3. Personally do you ever feel **seriously** bullied by any of the following this year? (Circle any or none of them)

Teaching staff   Students   Parents

Administrators

4. Do you think it is, or would be, a good idea? (Circle your answer)

a. To have a **specific policy** addressing bullying at the school	Yes	No
b. For teachers to talk to students about bullying	Yes	No
c. For students to be trained to be **peer helpers** to assist in countering bullying	Yes	No
d. For the **parents** of children involved in bully/victim problems to be interviewed by staff	Yes	No

5. Finally how serious do you think the problem of bullying in schools really is? (Circle your answer)

Very serious	Serious	Moderately serious	Not very serious	Not serious at all

QUESTIONNAIRE FOR PARENTS

We are interested in making sure that our school is a place where students can enjoy good relations with others. We want to know how you see your child relating to other students at school and in particular whether you think he or she ever experiences any bullying or harassment there. We would also appreciate your getting views on this matter. We have prepared this short questionnaire so that you can help us with our plans to ensure that this is a safe and happy school.

If you have more than one child at this school, please fill in a copy of this questionnaire for each child.

Sex of child _____ Age of child _____ Year of schooling_____

Would you say your child enjoys good relations with other students at school? (Check one)

      Yes, always or nearly always
      Usually does
      About half the time
      Usually does not
      Never or hardly ever

We may say children are being bullied if they are deliberately and repeatedly threatened or hurt by another person or group of people who are more powerful than themselves.

Would you say that your child has been bullied **this year** by a student or group of students in any of these ways? (Circle your answer)

By being threatened or physically hit	Never	Sometimes	Often
By being called unpleasant names	Never	Sometimes	Often
By being deliberately excluded	Never	Sometimes	Often

How has your child been affected by bullying this year? (Circle one)

      Not affected at all   Has been bothered by it   Has been upset by it

Has your child ever stayed home because of bullying? (Circle your answer)

      Never   For a day or so   For more than a day   I don't know

Do you think the school should have a specific anti-bullying policy? (Circle one)

      Yes   No   Unsure

Please add any comments you would like to make about the problem of bullying. We would welcome your opinion.

WARNING SIGNS THAT A CHILD IS BEING BULLIED AT SCHOOL

There are some signs that suggest that a child may be bullied at school. Parents should inquire as to whether the child is being bullied if these signs are present:

Physical   Unexplained bruises, scratches or cuts
                      Torn or damaged clothes or belongings

Psychosomatic   Non-specific pains, headaches, abdominal pains

Behavioural   Fear of walking to or from school
                      Change of route to school
                      Asking to be driven to school
                      Unwilling to go to school
                      Deterioration in school work
                      Coming home hungry (because lunch money was taken)
                      "Loss" of possessions/pocket money
                      Asking for or stealing money (to pay the bully)
                      Having few friends
                      Rarely invited to parties

                      Change in behaviour

                      Becomes withdrawn
                      Stammers
                      Has unexpected mood changes
                      Experiences irritability and temper outbursts
                      Appears upset, unhappy, tearful, distressed
                      Stops eating
                      Attempts suicide
                      Appears anxious: may wet bed, bite nails, seems afraid, develops tics, sleeps
                      poorly,   cries out in sleep
                      Refuses to say what is wrong
                      Gives improbable excuses or explanations for any of the above

From: Rigby, K. (1996). *Bullying in Schools and What to Do About It*, Markham, ON: Pembroke Publishers (adapted from Dr. Judith Dawkins).

BYSTANDER EXERCISE

Here is a picture of a person being bullied with a number of people watching. The person being pushed down is the **victim**; the person pushing the kid down is the **bully**.

1. How often does this kind of thing happen at your school? Place a tick under your answer.

Every day	Most days of the week	Once or twice a week	Less than once a week	Hardly ever
❏	❏	❏	❏	❏

2. Now please place a tick against what you think you would do if you were watching what was happening. Tick only one:

    ❏ I would ignore it

    ❏ I would support the person being pushed down

    ❏ I would support the person who is pushing the other kid down

    ❏ I would get a teacher

3. Write a sentence saying why you ticked the one you did.

    _____

    _____

    _____

    _____

    _____

DEFINING BULLYING

BULLYING INVOLVES:

a desire to hurt

+

hurtful action

+

a power imbalance

+

(typically) repetition

+

an unjust use of power

+

evident enjoyment by the aggressor

+

a sense of being oppressed on the part of the victim

QUIZ FOR STUDENTS ON BULLYING

Answer by circling "Agree" or "Unsure" or "Disagree" in each case.

Bullying is the same thing as fighting	Agree	Unsure	Disagree
Boys usually bully more than girls do	Agree	Unsure	Disagree
Kids who are not physically strong always get bullied	Agree	Unsure	Disagree
Telling someone you have been bullied usually makes things worse for you	Agree	Unsure	Disagree
Bullying mostly happens when there is no-one else around	Agree	Unsure	Disagree
Most bullying by boys is physical	Agree	Unsure	Disagree
Being bullied repeatedly can make a person depressed	Agree	Unsure	Disagree
Some children who have been severely bullied have taken their own lives	Agree	Unsure	Disagree
Calling people names can be bullying	Agree	Unsure	Disagree
Girls are more likely than boys to bully people by deliberately excluding them	Agree	Unsure	Disagree
One can always stop a person from bullying by hitting them back	Agree	Unsure	Disagree
Sometimes when you are being teased, it will stop if you ignore it	Agree	Unsure	Disagree
When students at school see bullying going on, they usually try to stop it	Agree	Unsure	Disagree
Bullies generally think badly of themselves	Agree	Unsure	Disagree
Some children are bullied because of their race	Agree	Unsure	Disagree
Some children are bullied because of some disability such as stammering	Agree	Unsure	Disagree
Schools can sometimes reduce bullying	Agree	Unsure	Disagree
Some children are more inclined to bully than others	Agree	Unsure	Disagree
Children who are bullied a lot tend to have few friends	Agree	Unsure	Disagree
Once a bully, always a bully	Agree	Unsure	Disagree

QUIZ FOR STUDENTS ON BULLYING (ANSWERS)

Bullying is the same thing as fighting	Agree	Unsure	**Disagree**
Boys usually bully more than girls do	**Agree**	Unsure	Disagree
Kids who are not physically strong always get bullied	Agree	Unsure	**Disagree**
Telling someone you have been bullied usually makes things worse for you	Agree	Unsure	**Disagree**
Bullying mostly happens when there is no-one else around	Agree	Unsure	**Disagree**
Most bullying by boys is physical	Agree	Unsure	**Disagree**
Being bullied repeatedly can make a person depressed	**Agree**	Unsure	Disagree
Some children who have been severely bullied have taken their own lives	**Agree**	Unsure	Disagree
Calling people names can be bullying	**Agree**	Unsure	Disagree
Girls are more likely than boys to bully people by deliberately excluding them	**Agree**	Unsure	Disagree
One can always stop a person from bullying by hitting them back	Agree	Unsure	**Disagree**
Sometimes when you are being teased, it will stop if you ignore it	**Agree**	Unsure	Disagree
When students at school see bullying going on, they usually try to stop it	Agree	Unsure	**Disagree**
Bullies generally think badly of themselves	Agree	Unsure	**Disagree**
Some children are bullied because of their race	**Agree**	Unsure	Disagree
Some children are bullied because of some disability such as stammering	**Agree**	Unsure	Disagree
Schools can sometimes reduce bullying	**Agree**	Unsure	Disagree
Some children are more inclined to bully than others	**Agree**	Unsure	Disagree
Children who are bullied a lot tend to have few friends	**Agree**	Unsure	Disagree
Once a bully, always a bully	Agree	Unsure	**Disagree**

THE BULLY/VICTIM CYCLE

BULLYING AND THE PASSIVE VICTIM

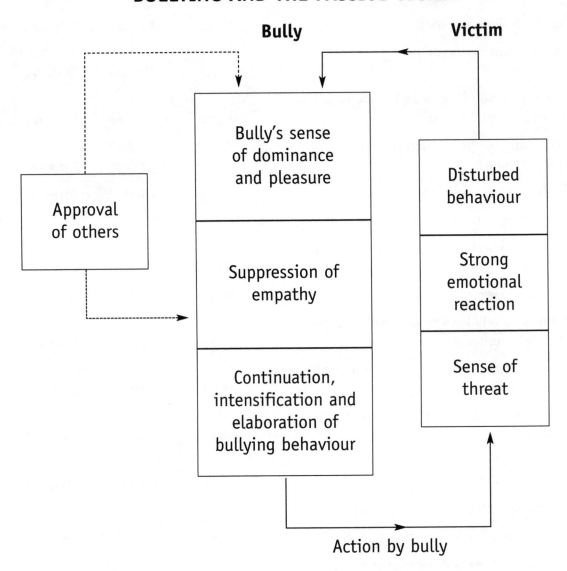

BULLYING AND THE RESISTANT VICTIM

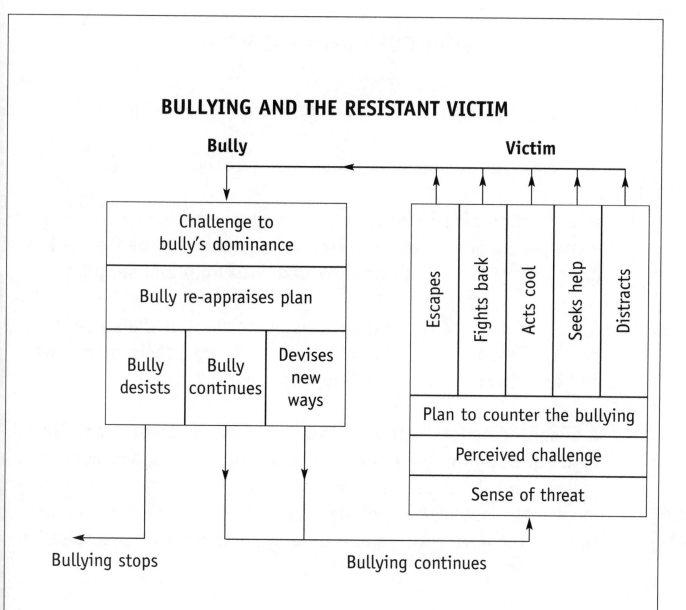

This diagram shows what victims often do to resist being bullied –
sometimes successfully, often not successfully.

WHAT GOES INTO THE POLICY

1. A strong statement of the **school's stand** against bullying.

2. A succinct **definition** of bullying, with illustrations.

3. A declaration of the **rights** of individuals in the school community – students, teachers, other workers and parents – **to be free of bullying** and (if bullied) **to be provided with help and support.**

4. A statement of the **responsibilities** of members of the school community: **to abstain personally from bullying** others in any way, and **to actively discourage bullying** when it occurs.

5. A **general** description of what the school will do **to deal with incidents of bullying.** For example, the severity and seriousness of the bullying will be assessed and appropriate action taken. This may include the use of counselling practices, the imposition of sanctions, interviews with parents and, in extreme cases, suspension from school.

6. An undertaking **to evaluate** the policy in the near and specified future.

ALTERNATIVE APPROACHES TO DEALING WITH BULLIES

1. **Providing and implementing clearly defined rules to apply appropriate "consequences" (or punishment) for those identified as having bullied someone.** These may range from loss of "privileges" or imposition of "chores", to detentions and suspension or exclusion from school.

2. **Counselling.** This may include **informal talks** with the bully who is seeking to change his or her behaviour. It could also involve a **more structured approach** of which two have been suggested:

    (i) **The No Blame Approach.** This requires groups of children containing the supposed bullies to be convened. Normally there would be a number of influential pro-social children involved. The plight of the victim is described and the group is left to come up with a responsible solution. The outcome is then carefully monitored.

    (ii) **The Method of Shared Concern.** This requires the counsellor to share his or her concern for the "victim" with individual members of the group and to elicit a promise to act in a specified and positive way in future interactions with the victim. This is done in a non-threatening manner along the lines suggested by Professor Anatol Pikas.

3. **School conferencing.** Bullies and victims are brought together at a meeting which their parents and friends also attend. Victims are strongly supported in expressing their objection to how they have been treated. The bully is induced to feel **a sense of shame** and is expected to make appropriate reparations before a reconciliation can be effected.

Note that what you do should depend upon:
  (i) **the sort of bully/victim problem** you have – e.g. its seriousness;
  (ii) **the school philosophy** on how change can best be produced; and
  (ii) a thorough understanding of **how each method works**.

TWENTY QUESTIONS TO ASK YOURSELF

Here are some questions you may like to address in discussions and in the course of providing a summary of how you think the problem of bullying should be addressed.

1. What consequences of bullying concern you most?
2. How satisfactory is the proposed definition of bullying? Can you improve on it?
3. What power inequalities does one have to accept in a school? What power differences at your school might be reduced and thereby minimise bullying?
4. What, if any, expressions of "forcefulness" in a school should be accepted or at least tolerated?
5. What means of bullying in your school would you most like to stop being exercised? How would you prioritise them?
6. At your school, what seem to be the main reasons why children bully?
7. What specific goals would you like to set for your school regarding bullying?
8. What components of the plan suggested in Section 17 would you mark as important for your school? Are there others you would add?
9. What steps do you think your school should take to get the facts about bullying at your school?
10. Is a school policy against bullying justified? If so, what should go into it? Who (staff, parents, students) should be included in helping to develop it?
11. How can teachers be guided and helped to raise the issue of bullying most effectively with their classes?
12. How can curriculum and lesson content help to raise awareness about bullying and help develop skills to counter it?
13. How can students become involved in initiating and taking positive action against bullying? Is forming a School Anti-Bullying Committee a good idea? What might it do? Should training in mediation and conflict resolution skills be provided? If so, how and by whom?
14. What kinds of resources (books and videos) would you recommend for the school to counter bullying?
15. How appealing are the alternative ways of dealing with cases of bullying? Under what circumstances, if any, would you see each of the ones suggested being employed? Is additional understanding and training in particular methods needed? If so, how can it be obtained?
16. Should the severity of the bullying and the reasons for the bullying behaviour be taken into account when dealing with the perpetrators?
17. How can children who bully be helped to lead more pro-social lives?
18. How can one ensure that children who are repeatedly victimised receive appropriate help, without matters being made worse?
19. How can one make sure that parents are included in the development of policy to counter bullying?
20. How can schools and parents best work together constructively when cases of bullying occur, and ensure the safety of children?